THIS, HERE, WILL LAST .

SUMAIYA

TO FAIZA, SAL AND YUMNA,

(MY NIECES AND NEPHEW WHO TAUGHT ME
TENDERNESS)

Contents

Preface — *vii*

Acknowledgements — *ix*

1. At 10 — 1

2. At 20 — 3

3. At 30 — 4

4. On Rough Patch — 5

5. Of Holding On — 6

6. At Her Threshold — 7

7. Of Staying Back — 8

8. Of Waiting. — 10

9. In Epiphanies — 11

10. To Giving In — 12

11. Of Mine — 13

12. Of Farewells — 14

13. On Home — 15

14. Of Nightmares — 16

15. On Endurance — 17

16. To Fall — 18

17. To Time Travel — 19

18. On Dooms — 21

19. To A Decade — 22

20. Of Meeting — 23

21. On Leaving — 24

22. Upon Staring — 25

Contents

23. On Second Coming   27

24. On Catching Up On Sleep   29

25. To Being Found   31

26. On Not Rushing   32

27. Of Noticing   33

Parting Thought   35

Preface

At different stages of my life, writing has meant different things. When I was younger and first started scribbling words that made sense only to me, it was because of reading, reading fascinated me. I wanted to have my own words to read, to own a few of them for myself. As I grew older, I discovered that I found expression more easily in writing than in speech. Poetry, though I still hesitate to call my musing, became a refuge I instinctively turned to. Often minor in the world's presence, and when I had no one to share what truly mattered with, I wrote.

Now, I'm older and have places to call home, spaces to share, I realise I have a voice that still trembles but has a calling. However, by now I have also registered that I am a forgetful person, and my mother is even more, and her mother is even more. Feelings, events, experiences, those rare and fleeting occurrences, joyful or painful, seldom repeat. I am afraid I will forget them once it has happened and pass, once it has left its footprints and left for good, like the wind that sways the dust on its way, I will fail to remember how deeply they moved me. So now when I write, it is to store, to stock what was felt, when it was felt. It is to pass down a life that was lived fully and partially.

This book holds a few of those articulated emotions from different phases of living. Lessons from the mundane moments that shaped me. Written in tender, reflective verse, these poems are offerings of quiet strength and vulnerable truths, capturing the subtle acts of endurance, belonging, and grace that define our most human moments.

I hope the warmth reaches you

Sumaiya

Acknowledgements

In the journey of bringing it to life, this book would not have been possible without the support of my family, whose quiet strength and love have held me steady. I am deeply grateful to my very lovely teachers, who sparked my love for words, backed me with unwavering encouragement and my friends, who stood by me in steady faith. A special mention to Vidhi, for being the gentle but persistent push I needed to begin this journey. And to Ayesha di, thank you for your honest affirmations, helping me believe in what I wrote. My loved one's belief gave my voice its courage.

1. At 10

Your recollection, an acute nostalgia.
Standing on no grounds,
Flapping through every call,
I envy you for belonging
To a time of peace.
You were unaware
That getting caught with fables
holds a sign.
Your head halting any approach,
Your scars only created from flogging.
I know it was never justified.
But as four summers will pass,
You shall learn to keep it for past.
Shimmering chances all around
But neither you cared to risk a try
Nor were you put to.
I wish you knew
As much as it is important
not to get hurt
Not to hurt was too.
Holding your lips like a dam
Perhaps for some people
You shall persist to be little.

Yet I will always remember you
By the meaning of your name,
For you were what you had to be.

2. At 20

Surreal to enter the third decade,
You are told to be living in a phase
called the spring of life.
But gracing back you realise:
It was all seasons combined,
Of highs that were actually low,
Of lows that fashioned highs.
Wanting to become a mountain
That stands firm with grace
I am unaware how it all started
How uncertainties left,
Defining you, your worth.
I may leave you untamed on some days,
But on most, I'm grateful I water you.
You are holding on to so many things
It's almost scary, you will tremble.
But haven't you stood enough
to stand this too?
Of all the things that remain,
This light of sacred warmth
Should never leave you.

3. At 30

Your name sounds synonyms
To expectations.
If I were to see you today,
I wish we exchange smiles, giggle
on the things only known to us
and depart, resting a content pat
on our shoulders.
You make me frightened,
You make me hopeful.
You stay in a world of could-bes,
And bring to life the best of possibilities.
Even if your scarf is wrinkled,
I always picture you with it.
Wherever the good hearts gather
and the good work is done.
If you truly exist, I hope you will know
There is more love to receive
And more places to visit.

4. On Rough Patch

When life was merciful,
Its pourings humbled me.
And when it was a downpour,
Greatest of arks didn't rescue me.
Perhaps,
Acceptance of every phase
makes you live, if you wish to live.
Whether it's the grace or the wrath
for mediocracy has long left the math.

5. Of Holding On

No smile I see reaches the eyes,
Or perhaps mine doesn't
Morning with all its lights-
Glistening colours, shimmers.
Everything delusional
Everything in its place,
Took away the worries
That were forged in broad daylight.
When night crept in
It sang from a scroll letter
Of all the wrongs
That could not be made right-
The labour taken
The hard-earned money
rained and then, dried
The homes, left
The tears, poured
The taunts, targeted
Not for a good end?
To take in all that
And to give in to this?

6. At Her Threshold

Often difficult to accept harsh decree
Often unbelievable to trust the process
the fate of the one
spent in distant from the excess
shedding generosity through her skin
striving and committed
she modestly forbore temptation,
carrying a load of ease for others
for her every action,
always an empathetic intervention
So how to console the soul
deserving utterly the best,
left to starve
of love, of little kindness
and maybe any little good.
Spiralling sleepless
questioning truth
The only provision to hold on to -
"perhaps you hate a thing
and it is good for you
and He knows,
while ye know not."

7. Of Staying Back

Going places I don't know,
existed
people I didn't know,
lived
displaced within me
confronting an air, proceeding me.
are you also hurt?
from the edges of yesterday
your worth, your worth
will plague your sleep
weigh on your conscience
maybe
richness surely defines one's path
yet I will live this mundane day
To breathe, to be
I will inherit this lonesome land
I will pass by these new faces
and a few old ones too
maybe I will get to know them more
maybe they will get to know me little
and when all has been wrapped
and all out of the way
there still will be time

to be raised
to be set free.

8. Of Waiting.

When did it become an obligation
I'm most freed here
but I cage myself
from entering its threshold
I blocked myself to savour
even when I know this is not filling
I have tired enough
tiring myself of waiting
I'm no longer sure
who will pay me heed
for my words are no more pearl bedded
no more of silken fabric
that left wonders at its touch
I am no starlight to fascinate
yesterday I replaced a stage
today the stage replaced me
with one closer to the sun.
I'm too stunned to be humble
I'm not too learned to be boastful
unaware of where these coloured words
will have to lead me.

9. In Epiphanies

Tittery walks
As thunderbolts lighten
the daylight
sprinkling life on
one hitherto dry
sight a few pastures
in the land of unknown
trace a few lives
of some are human
some inanimate
still more humane
there is a barrier
between the thing of beauty
and the eyes that quest it
it has always been
but never does the soul cease
to peep through it.
Never does it seek to impress.

10. To Giving In

• 12 •

Engulfed in cold breeze
shuttered by everything cold
reminded of all the warmth
that the now cold
had once caught hold.
these vessels of commend
these caskets of awe
enough to hold that what is hidden?
a colourless face
clenching remorse of greed
notwithstanding any replacement.
when things hasten to worse
Is it worthy of any preach ?

11. Of Mine

I'm making a concoction
of my mother's
forgetfulness and patience
my father is an alarmist
and articulation is
what he has for me
both tied in a single rope
of faith and humility,
am I spreading this potion
into the world for good,
or is it just building a rage
inside me?

12. Of Farewells

• 14 •

Thoughts filled in dimness
of partings
whose creation marked
as uncertain as two
trains collision
Is this another of my
proves to be human
and contain what is expected
to be humane
every road holds
something to let go
other things to hold onto
every passage demands
something to tear off
others to keep safe
of what grief and joy
tutored me,
in this ruckus called Life
what stays constant is change.

13. On Home

This is not a poem of triumph.
This is a poem of presence.
Of staying
when leaving was easier.
Of knowing
without needing to ask.
Of love,
in its strongest, quietest form.
Not just the bright mornings,
but the long, jagged nights.
There are grand declarations,
And there are no at all here.
But there is a truth that grows
quiet and wild between us,
like grass between cracks in stone.
I know if everything has to end
This, here, will last.

14. Of Nightmares

When night comes,
where does all the light go
The place that called
To tranquillity
Now is stained
With a sight
Transmitting cold-shivers
Inviting a corrupt heart
Was it always so easy
For "man" to be heinous
Will my worlds words
Or all the words of the world
Ever suffice
To make man give away it's lust
And make living easy?

15. On Endurance

Coping, a potion so traitorous
expecting the weak
to swim in happy
to not quiver
to not quest for respite
to hold the self, right
to push every last bit
to squeeze into
the whirlpool of achieving
when you are but only
being swept away-
in ache and hurt
at its finest curving

16. To Fall

The overwhelming rush
of sadness,
each time its in the door
it feels like
it has been here-
nameless
for what seems like
more than a lifetime.
Every time it stands
in my threshold
I shout that
my mother forbids
me to stand there
so you must step out.
Each time I cannot
breathe in this anxious head,
the subtle organ
almost declares
that there's no good left.
Each time I'm infected
I feel to be carrying
the loads in sprayers.

17. To Time Travel

What do you call it
when you vision
traversing back to the old
the crumbled old
the disliked old
the longing to become one, old
the dejected
and typically usual
fourteen-year-old.
It was sixteen when things
fell like taking place
rather falling into place
but waves after waves
with every forbearing days
I'm becoming a little wiser
and so,
a little sadder.
For now, what I do
is not a mere triumph
but what is just
expected of me.
So, maybe
as the seasons change

I leave for

my aboard for a warmer place

• 20 •

18. On Dooms

Doom,
when the crow, crows
then the dog, barks
and the dawn of intoxication
suddenly disappears.
And I tell you,
and you tell me-
this is all to pass
that we will hide in our shed
for as long as it lasts
that we hide ourselves
better, we do what they do
see how they see
silent the silence
breathe the air that they exhale
tell it's all fine
and one day one of us craves to be free,
that's when they shout
"Hide your identity"

19. To A Decade

before the accolades,
before I knew how to speak into rooms
Back when dreams were scribbles
on the last page of a notebook,
We were children.
but you looked at me like
I was already becoming.
As if the sweating palms
were not fear
but a spark.
When silence felt safer than speech
one quiet push at a time.
In your presence,
worth measured in upliftments
and bonds were treasured.
While I write myself forward,
I wish for joy to curl itself around you,
In a world that reflects back your light.

20. Of Meeting

I wish to meet you in the sea,
actually, beside it,
when the waves are in their equity,
I don't want you on the raft
and me on the shore.
I don't see myself in a seaside condo
and sight you trawling below.
Rather I want us seated on a bench
with warmth of sunrise at our glance,
the fresh sandy breeze of dawn
dirtied in our hands.
And room
unprocurable for arrogance to fit,
for we are the sea
and wave united in euphony.

21. On Leaving

And new places
Will remind you of old
And you will know
that it is not the place
But the feeling it ushered
Is what the old one did
And any place that succeeds
In doing so
Make sure you be in it.

22. Upon Staring

And then there are them
Less ornamented with glitters
More adorned with solitude
A remoteness brought about
By deceiving language
escalated ambitions
bounded limits
Mostly of the head
No one approaches such fate
What one does is grieve
To be able settle with being good.
I wonder
what it is to live with your plight
Living behind warmth of people
smiles that once crept on your height
light that beamed on your chest
Reassurance for a good time
Gratitude attached with one above
While this all ended you
to a biased world.
Your colour crimson, moss and black
Packed in your mother's care
Has fallen short of their standards

You say people came in pairs
While you wonder about
With steps lonely
I pray I see you in peaceful company.

23. On Second Coming

It's day
I walked out the nest
The sky says be:
Anything, but not depend
Unfurl your spirits
Learn your colours
Embrace your shades
Don't startle at your falls,
Nothing is a fall
Ancient Goodness
May not be your identity
So, clasp a hand of your choice
fall to fly
And nothing is really a fall
Your chaos, Your calm
Is for you to decide
Ancient Goodness
Calls present dainty.
The cage is calling, it is dusk
You walk back to your tree
The Nest's warmth still intact
A little damp with this new colour
A little wiser in this new fall

You are met with frowning eyes

Warm, comforting,

Exercising control

Enough to make you believe

The flight in the morning was wrong.

24. On Catching Up On Sleep

Warm breezy noon

Covered in a desired warmth

Intact in solitude,

a kind everyone, equally sharing

Sniffed in old books

Of new, of not in papers

In big and small screens

I read lines from one

Very brittle, very yellow

I tear its sides,

more than I understand it.

Slumber, slumber paving its path

Gingerly firming its grip

Resting my head I put all thoughts, down

All shadows casted towards me, away

Free from all harshness

Eyes shut in kind rest

Oh how delicate solace

bodies are capable of inviting

Beauty is in being

how complete to sense events.

So, this is what flesh need

Soul, heart, head and feelings
Have their own affairs inclined
But for the body it is
On a warm breezy noon
Covered in a desired warmth
Intact in silence
Catching up on sleep

25. To Being Found

the subtle colors in this image
Like the pastels we are holding
the pink gazing from the back
holding all things delicately
Golden hour of the sun
Resting on our hands,
Already warm in the other's presence.
Yours, leaning
Just the right amount to tell I'm not forlorn.
Mine, firmly facing
A promise to never move away
If asked truly to stay.

26. On Not Rushing

Staring at the blinking blaze,
Lightened far away
Keeping someone warm,
While relishing the call to success
I sit stunned.
Mundane things all around
Yet perceiving everything
And commenting on none
It dawned on me,
All things
keep up with grace.

27. Of Noticing

And I should register,
falling of confetti from trees
light scream of a little girl
I'm not related to.
plight of the limping
The joy boxed in grooving
The pain of forged care
Delight in new episodes
Often Grey, otherwise pink
Seek to pursue the feeling
Even if nothing
consumes you entirely
riding in this wave
perhaps life's beauty
will overweigh its pain

Parting Thought

Thank you for holding my words in your hands and heart. Your time, presence, and attention mean the world. I'm deeply grateful we could meet here, even briefly. Leaving you in the care of The Almighty.

في أمان الله

"Love wears butterflies on the ends of her Hijab, and will remove her glasses to blur out the world...love lives all across India, but for now its living in your heart"

- Samriddhi